WHAT SHOULD THE U.S. ARMY LEARN FROM HISTORY? RECOVERY FROM A STRATEGY DEFICIT

Colin S. Gray

U.S. ARMY WAR COLLEGE
SSI
STRATEGIC STUDIES INSTITUTE

The United States Army War College

The United States Army War College educates and develops leaders for service at the strategic level while advancing knowledge in the global application of Landpower.

The purpose of the United States Army War College is to produce graduates who are skilled critical thinkers and complex problem solvers. Concurrently, it is our duty to the U.S. Army to also act as a "think factory" for commanders and civilian leaders at the strategic level worldwide and routinely engage in discourse and debate concerning the role of ground forces in achieving national security objectives.

The Strategic Studies Institute publishes national security and strategic research and analysis to influence policy debate and bridge the gap between military and academia.

The Center for Strategic Leadership contributes to the education of world class senior leaders, develops expert knowledge, and provides solutions to strategic Army issues affecting the national security community.

The Peacekeeping and Stability Operations Institute provides subject matter expertise, technical review, and writing expertise to agencies that develop stability operations concepts and doctrines.

The School of Strategic Landpower develops strategic leaders by providing a strong foundation of wisdom grounded in mastery of the profession of arms, and by serving as a crucible for educating future leaders in the analysis, evaluation, and refinement of professional expertise in war, strategy, operations, national security, resource management, and responsible command.

The U.S. Army Heritage and Education Center acquires, conserves, and exhibits historical materials for use to support the U.S. Army, educate an international audience, and honor Soldiers—past and present.

STRATEGIC STUDIES INSTITUTE

The Strategic Studies Institute (SSI) is part of the U.S. Army War College and is the strategic-level study agent for issues related to national security and military strategy with emphasis on geostrategic analysis.

The mission of SSI is to use independent analysis to conduct strategic studies that develop policy recommendations on:

- Strategy, planning, and policy for joint and combined employment of military forces;

- Regional strategic appraisals;

- The nature of land warfare;

- Matters affecting the Army's future;

- The concepts, philosophy, and theory of strategy; and,

- Other issues of importance to the leadership of the Army.

Studies produced by civilian and military analysts concern topics having strategic implications for the Army, the Department of Defense, and the larger national security community.

In addition to its studies, SSI publishes special reports on topics of special or immediate interest. These include edited proceedings of conferences and topically oriented roundtables, expanded trip reports, and quick-reaction responses to senior Army leaders.

The Institute provides a valuable analytical capability within the Army to address strategic and other issues in support of Army participation in national security policy formulation.

Strategic Studies Institute

and

U.S. Army War College Press

WHAT SHOULD THE U.S. ARMY LEARN FROM HISTORY?
RECOVERY FROM A STRATEGY DEFICIT

Colin S. Gray

July 2017

The views expressed in this report are those of the author and do not necessarily reflect the official policy or position of the Department of the Army, the Department of Defense, or the U.S. Government. Authors of Strategic Studies Institute (SSI) and U.S. Army War College (USAWC) Press publications enjoy full academic freedom, provided they do not disclose classified information, jeopardize operations security, or misrepresent official U.S. policy. Such academic freedom empowers them to offer new and sometimes controversial perspectives in the interest of furthering debate on key issues. This report is cleared for public release; distribution is unlimited.

*****

This publication is subject to Title 17, United States Code, Sections 101 and 105. It is in the public domain and may not be copyrighted.

*****

Comments pertaining to this report are invited and should be forwarded to: Director, Strategic Studies Institute and U.S. Army War College Press, U.S. Army War College, 47 Ashburn Drive, Carlisle, PA 17013-5010.

*****

This manuscript was funded by the U.S. Army War College External Research Associates Program. Information on this program is available on our website, *ssi.armywarcollege.edu*, at the Opportunities tab.

*****

All Strategic Studies Institute (SSI) and U.S. Army War College (USAWC) Press publications may be downloaded free of charge from the SSI website. Hard copies of certain reports may also be obtained free of charge while supplies last by placing an order on the SSI website. Check the website for availability. SSI publications may be quoted or reprinted in part or in full with permission and appropriate credit given to the U.S. Army Strategic Studies Institute and U.S. Army War College Press, U.S. Army War College, Carlisle, PA. Contact SSI by visiting our website at the following address: *ssi.armywarcollege.edu*.

*****

The Strategic Studies Institute and U.S. Army War College Press publishes a quarterly email newsletter to update the national security community on the research of our analysts, recent and forthcoming publications, and upcoming conferences sponsored by the Institute. Each newsletter also provides a strategic commentary by one of our research analysts. If you are interested in receiving this newsletter, please subscribe on the SSI website at the following address: *ssi.armywarcollege.edu /newsletter/*.

FOREWORD

What is commonly known as history is really the past, as it is often selected and preserved both by professional historians and by non-specialist citizens. The past is such a large and diverse repository of happenings, thoughts, and experiences that it requires treatment with a disciplined respect. Frequently, respect for the truth about the past is a victim of contemporary circumstance. In this monograph, Dr. Colin S. Gray seeks to explore how historical data might best be used for the benefit of the U.S. Army and, therefore, the United States. He pulls no punches in explaining how challenging it is to penetrate the fog that obscures much of the past. Since the future cannot be foreseen reliably, we are left rather uncomfortably with a seemingly ever changing today.

Despite the difficulties that are soon found by efforts to identify lessons from history, Dr. Gray does believe there are a few major precepts to which respectful attention should be paid. For example, he states and argues in this monograph that the decision to wage war is always a gamble, despite the many advantages owned by the United States in most circumstances. In particular, thinking especially of such unhappy protracted episodes as the conduct of warfare in Vietnam, Afghanistan, and Iraq, the work is impressed by the extent and depth of the American lack of knowledge and understanding of combat zones. The author hopes that this modest study will help American soldiers cope with the huge scope and mass of potential data from the relevant past.

DOUGLAS C. LOVELACE, JR.
Director
Strategic Studies Institute and
    U.S. Army War College Press

ABOUT THE AUTHOR

COLIN S. GRAY is Professor Emeritus of International Politics and Strategic Studies at the University of Reading, England. He worked at the International Institute for Strategic Studies in London, England, and at the Hudson Institute in Croton-on-Hudson, New York, before founding the National Institute for Public Policy, a defense-oriented think tank in the Washington, DC, area. Dr. Gray served for 5 years in the Ronald Reagan administration on the President's General Advisory Committee on Arms Control and Disarmament. A dual citizen of the United States and the United Kingdom, he has served as an adviser to both the U.S. and British Governments. His government work has included studies of nuclear strategy, arms control, maritime strategy, space strategy, and special forces. Dr. Gray has written 29 books, including: *The Sheriff: America's Defense of the New World Order* (University Press of Kentucky, 2004); *Another Bloody Century: Future Warfare* (Weidenfeld and Nicolson, 2005); *Strategy and History: Essays on Theory and Practice* (Routledge, 2006); *Fighting Talk: Forty Maxims on War, Peace and Strategy* (Potomac Books, 2009); *National Security Dilemmas: Challenges and Opportunities* (Potomac Books, 2009); *The Strategy Bridge: Theory for Practice* (Oxford University Press [OUP], 2010); *War, Peace and International Relations: An Introduction to Strategic History*, 2nd Ed. (Routledge, 2011); *Airpower for Strategic Effect* (Air University Press, 2012); and *Perspectives on Strategy* (OUP, 2013), which is the follow-on to *Strategy Bridge*. The final volume in the *Strategy Bridge* trilogy, entitled *Strategy and Defence Planning: Meeting the Challenge of Uncertainty*, was published by OUP in 2014. Dr. Gray is a graduate of the Universities of Manchester and Oxford.

SUMMARY

This monograph examines the potential utility of history as a source of education and possible guidance for the U.S. Army. The author considers the worth in the claim that since history (more accurately termed the past) is all done and gone, it can have no value for today as we try to look forward. This point of view did not find much favor here. The monograph argues that although history does not repeat itself in detail, it certainly does so roughly in parallel circumstances. Of course, much detail differs from one historical case to another, but nonetheless, there are commonly broad and possibly instructive parallels that can be drawn from virtually every period of history, concerning most circumstances.

An argument that finds very little favor here is that attracted to claims for the value of assertions of historical analogy. This monograph suggests that the strict requirements for detailed evidence that is required for credible claims of analogy are effectively impossible to meet. Since it can be important not to lose all grasp of the comparison, the idea—perhaps the habit— of claiming historical analogy should be dropped. Instead, a much more useful concept that avoids the error of foolish analogy is the idea of the historical parallel. The parallel claim conveys the core of the analogical one, while expediently saving us from the need to try to make claims that are bound to exceed the accessible evidence.

We explore and carefully consider the popular idea expressed by writer L. P. Hartley half a century ago that "the past is a foreign country." This idea is important and remains quite popular, but it does not withstand careful criticism. Controversially, I am sure this monograph, though recognizing and welcoming much change in world affairs, is unconvinced that truly major themes in human political and spiritual life have altered significantly over the centuries. While nearly all of the detail and what may be termed dismissively as the decorative and even mechanical features of private and public life have changed greatly over the past 2 centuries, the values of morality, politics, and the connections between effort and reward, have not really altered at all. For a leading example, the standard and traditional formula of ends, ways, and means (and assumptions) works for the interpretation of all cultures, in all periods of history. The reason is because the interdependence of the four vital ideas, at all times and in all circumstances, enjoys the rare status of being a truth for the whole human race, and it is an important key for unlocking the details of many disparate civilizations.

The analysis here is not unfriendly to the idea of change, but it is unimpressed with many claims for alteration that are not, in fact, evidence of radical improvement. Unsurprisingly, perhaps, relatively little with the highest value for human life is found to have changed over a long passage of time. By way of empirical evidence for this argument, the aspirations and achievements, as well as many of the crimes, as we might choose to label them, continue to make sense to us. It is impressive that three of the four greatest books on war, statecraft, and strategy were written millennia in the past, while the most outstanding book on land warfare, by Carl von Clausewitz, was first published 184 years ago.

Among the conclusions reached in this analysis is the important thought that history teaches no lessons—it is historians who do that. The study reaches four significant conclusions; they are the following:

1. Behave prudently (meaning with regard for the consequences of action).
2. Remember the concept of the great stream of time.
3. Do not forget that war nearly always is a gamble.
4. War should only be waged with strategic sense.

WHAT SHOULD THE U.S. ARMY LEARN FROM HISTORY? RECOVERY FROM A STRATEGY DEFICIT

INTRODUCTION: SHOULD THE U.S. ARMY LEARN FROM HISTORY?

It is my contention that the late British author and dramatist, L. P. Hartley, was substantially in error when he offered audiences the potent thought that "the past is a foreign country: they do things differently there."[1] It is an assumption for this monograph that history offers much from which the U.S. Army could learn. However, this analysis approaches the injunction in the title principally as a hypothesis to be tested, rather than as a great and solemnly reliable truth. The trouble is that there is no such thing as history. History is what historians write, and historians are part of the process they are writing about as well.[2] The Hartley quote is particularly instructive for two reasons. First, it offers a very plausible common thought that today approaches the status of being an all but revealed truth that speaks sense to a common error. Second, in the opinion of this scholar, Hartley is seriously mistaken in his understanding of history, at least in the level of his understanding, which I deem to be somewhat shallow. That said, the facts remain that Hartley's striking thought and particularly his choice of words merits our serious attention and even much respect. There is a notable plausibility about Hartley's phrase-making that commands attention. In short, he expresses what reads like a well-considered conviction resting upon an impressive pile of historical evidence! However, we ought to ask: Is it true? — notwithstanding its apparent plausibility.

A prior question must be posed before one seeks to tackle this topic. An unavoidable issue of legitimacy precedes that of topicality. Is it sensible simply to assume that history carries meaning for us today? The idea of our learning from whatever we decide history to be deserves to be regarded as a proposition for disciplined consideration, not as a matter that already is comfortably settled. Our past is not only one with a dynamic national boundary, but also one that both has, and provides context for, the national narratives of other peoples. It is not hard to see how complex the idea of history rapidly can become.

Fortunately, this monograph is designed to answer a particular need of the U.S. Army for specific advice on what should be learned from history. An obvious problem here is the need to decide on a rule for the education in question. Common sense must be our practical guide, even though it requires toleration of unpoliced intellectual frontiers. A large and general issue could be, but will not be, debated here. Specifically, there is a highly significant difference between history and the past. In popular discussion, and also unfortunately in professional scholarship, history is the human story usually framed and drafted to promote a specific narrative, and the past is simply the real story of what happened, why, and to whom. The latter concept is close in reality to the early medieval chronicles. By and large, authors today have a point of view that they wish to project, and we live in a society that permits this. The subject of this monograph may appear unmanageably broad, but in reality, one assumes that authors debating the proper valuable use of historical evidence will be guided in detail by a set of assumptions. These assumptions will be believed both to be widely shared within American society, and endorsed by the institutions licensing the research, writing, and dissemination of the view expressed. It is plausible to argue that monographs written for the educational purposes of the U.S. Army are near certain to reflect assumptions friendly to concerns for national security. A possible lack of objectivity is not really relevant to my argument, because I am stating a necessary truth. When we learn from our history, there is no avoiding the consequences of the particular details that, as individuals, we cannot help but bring to the exercise. It can be a challenge for scholars, including those who attempt to educate soldiers more fully, to avoid permitting bias to defeat education.

Soldiers, among many others, may learn from the history that they are taught that the righteous side did not always win. This possible judgment ought not to disturb students who already have been introduced to the culturally challenging notion that America could and did lose some wars, or at least some phases of particular wars—even if the whole wartime narration is more kind. Military students in most countries know that defeats happen occasionally, and they learn that the whole course of national military history is not one of unblemished success. Indeed, it is important for an institution that seeks to teach the national strategic narrative to be able to teach also the facts concerning occasional military failure. Historically, American soldiers have needed to be educated by the reality of failure as well as victory. From time to time, especially when introduced into what becomes the late stage of a war, the U.S. Army has been seriously short of combat skills—at least for a brief period.[3] For example, a German enemy provided rapid on the job training.

From time to time, historical judgements are presented and quite plausibly rejected as irrelevant. A principal problem is created not by the appeal to what is claimed to be history, but much rather by the careful selection of episodes in the past on which the requirements for evidence are levied. While it is commonplace to reject possible and potential evidence of sound or apparently unsound behavior, it is not usually feasible to evade the problem created by our foreknowledge entirely. This is probably the oldest and least forgiving of authorial sins. Specifically, we know what happened and cannot pretend convincingly that we do not. When a complete historical narrative is well known, it is tempting simply to ignore the possibly glittering paths that were not explored. A professional historian generally will not touch interesting plot inventions adopted even for the purpose of illustrating of an argument judged worthy of presentation, explanation, and augmentation. If an author chooses to liven up their narrative, he or she may lose the necessary anchor of well-evidenced actuality that helps keep him or her from slipping into the realm of fiction. As it is, the interdependence of fiction and non-fiction can pose a significant challenge to an understanding of the past, without inviting a new source of fiction to join the party. This author has never felt compelled to use deliberate fiction in order to strengthen an argument. I have always felt that the uncertainties of contemporary strategic fiction were sufficiently exciting as not to need colorful embellishment.

The utility argument in praise of research on the future rapidly runs into the venture stopping problem that, since the future by scientific definition has yet to happen, it is quite a challenge to assess any weight of evidence in (self) praise of one's own foresight! Fortunately, we are not quite as blind on the future as I may have just appeared to suggest. Nonetheless, the nature and number of genuine certainties is quite limited, despite their high significance.

Perhaps the most helpful thought one can offer on the likely value of history for our security tomorrow is the following: today is only tomorrow's yesterday. If nothing else, it should encourage a rare humility in futurologists.

UNDERSTANDING THE PAST: A FOREIGN COUNTRY?

This belief is as popular, even if often regretted, as actually it is exceedingly dubious. The differences from past to present and on into the future certainly are considerable, but often they tend not to relate to the deeper phenomena that bear on our human performance. There is a good and readily understandable reason why this should be so. Specifically, for reasons of personal security, we human beings find it necessary to live in groups, or societies, great or small in size. In order to live with tolerable security in a society — any society — we need guidance as to the distinction between acceptable and unacceptable behavior. The group, or society if you prefer, into which we all happen to be born, in every contemporary political geography and also in every known period in history, finds it necessary to instruct its children about the difference between rightful and wrongful behaviors. Similarly, all people, everywhere, are subject to parental and societal influence.

Over millennia and in very different geographies, most peoples, certainly the socially and politically successful ones, have been able to adapt to what could prove to be challenging geographical and human political and strategic conditions. However, extreme conditions of stress have not generally resulted in truly extreme consequences of a kind that repudiated what went before. Even when there have been noteworthy violent interruptions to the normal conditions of civilized life, one finds that the most obvious changes in political, social, and military affairs are less traumatic than appeared the case on a more superficial assessment. The more closely we examine, and the more broadly we consider the past, the more familiar it seems with reference to our contemporary times.

A trap we need to be careful to try to avoid is the drawing of powerful sweeping conclusions based on singular, outstanding, and quite possibly unusual historical happenings. In short, we need to try to avoid being over-impressed by individual, perhaps stand alone, occurrences or even inventions. The argument that advances the potent proposition that the past is a foreign country is true in the main, but there are important respects in which the argument should be dismissed as a plausible fallacy. Of particular interest is the subject of human behavior and misbehavior. This author has often been impressed by the similarities between contemporary people and those in the time of Ancient Greece and Rome.[4] While there can be no doubt that imperial politics in the Roman Empire could have a distinctly rough edge for the losers in power struggles, the probable motivation and temptations appear substantially comprehensible to today.

The range of possibility in human physiology and psychology has not altered dramatically through the centuries. If that were not so, we should probably not be able to read Thucydides' *History of the Peloponnesian War* with much understanding of the politics, tactics, operations, and strategies it seeks to explain.[5] Not only is Thucydides' book the outstanding work from a period of intense intercity strife 2,400 years in the past, but particularly when well translated from the challenging Greek-style in which it was written, it speaks clearly to us today. Former Secretary of State General George C. Marshall argued that one could not be a fully competent contemporary observer of international politics if one were not familiar with Thucydides.[6] Of course, fashions, habits, and legally permissible tactics, operations, and strategies have changed over the centuries, but the morality theme in the human tale has not altered unrecognizably.[7] The stories in Shakespeare's plays that are set in times even then long past do not require translation for today, any more than do his late 16th-century plays.

Probably the most difficult challenge one needs to face in striving to make moral, social, political, and strategic sense of historical figures is the need to attempt to understand the largely silent assumptions made by them.[8] It is in the nature and character of assumptions that typically they contain or imply beliefs that do not require explicit justification or even expression. We function day to day on the basis of assumptions, as did all the historical figures in whom we have an interest. An assumption is a belief that is accepted as true, even though the evidence on its behalf may be shaky at best. A common problem posed to historians by the phenomenon of the assumption is the widespread reality of a genuine lack of self-knowledge in its respect. An assumption can be regarded as a belief in support of which we have not sought persuasive evidence. An assumption is a belief that is beyond, or even above, evidence. By their nature, assumptions pose tough challenges to the historian. It can be a difficult idea to convey to young people, because it challenges the scientific spirit of our era. When properly explained, much, though not all, of the difficulty vanishes. The challenge lies in the requirement to believe, or at least accept, that particular claims are true, or likely to be true enough, in the face of a lack of what usually is understood as supportive evidence. Emphatically, this does not mean that an assumption is wrong, only that it is not supported by what is regarded as tolerably accurate evidence. The understanding of what should be considered accurate evidence typically requires effort and empirical results.

An understanding of assumptions is important because all human behavior—past, present, and presumably future—is driven by people who cannot help making and holding them. Assumptions are crucially significant for our values, moral compass, and choices. The historical experience from which we expect and require American soldiers to be both inspired and warned is shot through with collective, but also individual, distinctively moral choices between better and worse behavior. Students of history, both national and foreign, learn at a young age that they inhabit and must conduct themselves in a society founded upon a code of what is regarded as morally acceptable behavior. When studying history, the student is introduced to a wide spread of behaviors that the teacher will explain either in generally positive or negative terms. Students probably will not recognize the reality of their situation, but that context will always be a moral one. Students will be exposed to both more and less successful examples of the human experience, but regardless of the details of time and place, the teacher will be explaining about a morally structured world. The students always will be taught the differences between positive and negative performances, both collective and individual. Regardless if one is studying

Thucydides or Julius Caesar, the relevant universe for action in history is a moral one. Ideas, standards, and laws have varied widely, but we humans have always found it necessary to endorse an ethical code expressing notions of morally acceptable behavior.

PERSISTING CONCERNS AND ENDURING HAZARDS

In order for a false belief to be exposed as a fallacy, it first needs to be recognized as seriously flawed. Only then, once expressed to public view and possibly confronted with contrary empirical evidence, can the truth be established. The most obvious difficulty with falsity of assumptions for soldiers and their political masters is that prediction is a notably uncertain activity in human political and strategic affairs. This condition of uncertainty is particularly acute for America's soldiers, given that the most crucial aspects of their professional readiness all but require them to achieve the impossible with anticipation of the future. Given that reliable prediction of the future is not a physical, mechanical, or electronic possibility for us, we need to examine our history in a search for guidance on prudent international behavior.[9]

Sometimes it is a dominant truth in international politics that the United States ought not to be cast in the role of principal actor, meaning that foreign concerns and decisions lead the way in deciding when, and possibly where, the country is moved to commit to violent action. Regarding the whole of the 20th century, we were ready neither for the World Wars (1917, 1941) nor for the limited ones (1950, 1965, and 2001). The country hoped to be able to sit out both World Wars, but that proved impossible. The falsehood of

American assumptions about its international context and prudent choices was revealed fairly conclusively in 1917 and yet more so in 1941. It soon became obvious that the political assumptions upon the basis of which military policy was founded were unsound. The most popular beliefs about the country's national security were erroneous both in 1917 and 1941. More arguably, perhaps, the Truman administration, which enjoys almost a stellar reputation today for its eventual management of Soviet peril concerning the balance of power in Europe and much of Asia, was caught unprepared over nuclear weapons both materially and conceptually in Korea in 1950.

The most serious weakness in the American way of war since World War II has been what deserves to be labeled the strategy deficit.[10] The theory of strategy is almost brutally clear in the emphasis it places upon the political meaning that there needs to be to all warfighting, actual or potential.[11] Admittedly, the problem is a political one for the whole of American national security, not a narrow challenge solely to the American conduct of war. Repeatedly in armed conflicts in the second half of the 20th century and the opening decade of the 21st, the United States waged war (in Vietnam, Afghanistan, and Iraq) with too little effort being devoted to the whole narrative and context of conflict. A U.S. military effort and the political energy that it generated should have learned from history that warfare is always really about politics and must have political consequences. This was true for Ancient Greece and Rome, neither less nor more than for the contemporary United States. Strict logic, common sense, and abundant historical experience should be allowed to tell us that what strategy is about are the consequences of military action or sometimes inaction.

It can be difficult to bear this point in mind, but all military behavior has some political meaning, great or small. Military behavior in times of peace and of war always has political consequences, both anticipated or not and desired or otherwise.

Just as military use always has consequences — ones less than accurately anticipated — they are frequently surprising. This is a plain generically repeated lesson from most historical experiences. The root problem, of course, is the unpredictability of the future. The pertinent challenge to us is to identify the elements in history that bear significantly upon the security and general well-being of the American people, but which are not unduly vulnerable to thoughts and actions that malign individuals and institutions. This is a tough but not impossible task, hence the feasibility of this monograph. In a later section of this monograph, I risk identifying the lessons that American soldiers can and should derive from their study of history — not just American history. Prominent among these lessons is the condition that well merits the title used in this monograph, a strategy deficit. The problem has not been especially difficult to identify, but it has been nearly impossible to correct. The very structure of American governance, with the constitutional protection of a separation of powers, almost guarantees a probability of considerable difficulty with respect to the provision of a sound balancing of ends, ways, and means. Strategy is by far the most challenging activity, as contrasted with policy and military tactics, so it is no surprise that it has posed difficulties that are unusual in their severity. This unremarkable conclusion was reached in a recent major study by the RAND Corporation. Attempting to summarize why the American national security effort over the past 13 years has been unsatisfactory, the study argued the following:

> First, civilian policymakers and the U.S. military have different conceptions of how policy and strategy should be made. Second, policymakers have a tendency to eschew strategy and focus on tactical issues. Third, and perhaps most important, is a desire to pursue a technocratic approach to strategy that aligns tactical and operational successes without securing the ultimate objectives sought. Finally, policymakers and military leaders may not see strategy as an essentially adaptive art for coping with the uncertainties of war and the lack of perfect knowledge. A significant body of scholarship has identified these issues, and some effort has been made to increase and improve education in strategy, but a wider appreciation of the degree to which this deficit produces suboptimal national security outcomes may be lacking.[12]

With the advance in military-relevant technology as the leading contemporary example, we know that it has to be a reliably safe bet for us to anticipate a continuation of the still maturing digital revolution. Historical experience cannot advise as to which technical and behavioral solutions should and will find most favor with the Army in the future, but we can be totally confident in expecting adequate answers to be located. Looking forward to yet an even more digital age (and beyond), the study of history tells us that the age-old competition between technical offense and defense is certain to continue. After all, since such competition, if sometimes very slow, has been characteristic literally for millennia, why should it stop now? There is, and will never be, a final technical move (that we could survive). The pace of technical change accelerates and decelerates, driven substantially by appreciation of perceived acute military need. The only technology to date to have evaded reliably certain technical negation is the weaponization of atomic energy.[13] However, American soldiers, among others, can hardly have avoided noticing that for the 72 years since Hiroshima and Nagasaki, nuclear weapons have played a notable background role on behalf of American national security. The point is not that nuclear weapons do not much matter, which would be far from the truth, but rather that typically they are allowed to play little part in America's explicit statecraft. They are uniquely valuable, indeed literally indispensable, but they appear to have played only a key contextual role. This is not a criticism; long may nuclear-armed forces be assigned only a background role! The answer to the technical challenge posed by nuclear weapons has been consistently clear. We accept nuclear weapons as having a prospectively permanent character as a military threat to which there is no thoroughly reliable solution for negation. Since the mid–1950s, we have accepted a condition of mutual deterrence as being the best, indeed the only, solution to the military problems posed by Soviet nuclear-armed forces. The danger posed by a small number of nuclear weapons has meant that even warfare on behalf of vital interests has acquired an all but impossible quality of risk. However, this condition of acute danger, with nuclear peril overhanging great-power politics, has had an arguably surprisingly limited effect on America's military activity. Korea, Vietnam, Afghanistan, and Iraq, assayed cumulatively have been extensive enterprises. I am tempted to comment that for a nuclear well-armed superpower, the United States, and its Army in particular, has had a busy and indeed a hard and trying time.

Modern history tells us that the United States lost its wars in Vietnam, and probably Afghanistan and Iraq. It is hard to maintain credibly that American backed arms were proven undoubtedly successful in recent conflicts. So much for the unsatisfactory military historical record. On the plus side of the historical ledger we must record the successful defense of South Korea and, above all else, the framing and persistent execution of a defense strategy for the North Atlantic Treaty Organization (NATO) countries of Western Europe. It is perhaps ironic that America's greatest success in the field of competitive international security was in Western and Central Europe, where nuclear dangers were most acute. The scale of danger may have promoted prudence, but still history must record a bold, successful, and vital nuclear grand strategy effected largely by the United States. Today, the Soviet peril has been at least partially born again in the unpleasant character of the new authoritarian Russia under Vladimir Putin. In addition, the hazards in mutual nuclear deterrence continue to lurk, possibly in dark unpredictable corners, and thereby, especially in dangerous ways.

In conflict after conflict, the U.S. military establishment, alongside its many strengths, has revealed the same weakness—in strategy. As is well known, there is not or should not be a need for savior generalship, or indeed other extraordinary performance. The persisting problem is that the military, the U.S. Army in particular, has failed to heed well what it teaches itself in its institutions of higher military education about the virtues of strategy. When strategy is neglected or impossible, tactics and operations are not connected to what ought to be understood as their purpose. Ulysses Grant understood this basic point in 1864; it was the most effective reason why the Civil War ended how and when it did. Grant fought purposefully; unfortunately, U.S. military action for several decades has not been close to being so well-led.[14]

A FAMILIAR PAST? PARALLELS AND ANALOGIES

Erroneous analogy is one of many blights to which users of English may fall victim.[15] At its best, analogy aids understanding by means of the simple linguistic trick of changing one topic in debate from a subject on which you are not well versed, to one for which you are much better prepared. The explicit or implicit similarity in some potentially significant degree between the two cases legitimizes the introduction of analogy. The use and frequent abuse of analogy is commonplace in public political life. After all, there is little that is authentically novel in our politics. Times and their particular issues certainly alter, but all human emotions and the pertinent moral, immoral, and amoral urges that move people to and away from particular behaviors persist. They do not seem to have changed much for centuries, probably millennia. Love and hatred, loyalty and treachery, honesty and dishonesty, design and accident and so forth, are prominent in the list of large binaries. These pairings comprise a formidable short list of the values and sentiments that we believe demarcate us from the rest of the animal world.

One can contrast the idea of the historical parallel with that of the historical analogy. Readers are advised, perhaps alerted, and warned that this author is not in favor of the use of what are claimed to be historical analogies. In many years of scholarship, I have found the idea of the historical parallel far more useful. The two standards under discussion here, analogy and parallel, are closely related, but there is a critically individualizing distinction that renders the concept of a parallel far safer to use than that of analogy. Specifically, the concept of a parallel is much looser than is that of analogy. Although both ideas claim to rest upon notable similarities between subjects, the claim on behalf of alleged parallelism is considerably weaker than is that required to support a credible claim for analogy. This is not to suggest formally that proof of common identity is required on behalf of the argument favoring analogy. When historians make claims to understand similar seeming societies, they should appreciate that the evidence advanced is likely to be regarded with heavy suspicion. It may be vulnerable even to evidence of single-point nonconformity. It is commonplace for authors who want to argue boldly on the authority of asserted analogy; really, they mean to claim only that most or many, rather than strictly all cases are what they have in mind.

For the same reason that most, if not quite all, claims for paradox should be more accurately understood as ones for irony, so nearly all claims for the virtue in analogy would be composed more accurately were they confined to arguments on behalf of parallelism. The idea of the historical parallel captures the principal aspect of the idea of analogy, while avoiding the need for strict similarity or even identity. A leading reason why the assertions of analogy should be resisted is that its claims are—and indeed should be—assumed to cover cases that really are like-for-like. The trouble with this rigorous, but fair requirement to demand of claims for historical analogy, is that it is incompatible with the rich variety of human life and experience. Of course, there are significant seeming similarities between individuals, institutions, and experiences, including many that are centuries, even millennia, apart. However, possibly without exception, the individual historical context will prove on close examination to contain particular individual human, societal-cultural, and institutional detail that is sufficiently unique for us to be uneasy as scholars, should we seek to homogenize disparate people and their circumstances too rigorously.

An advantage of parallels over analogies is that the former require only the plausible evidence of there being strong similarities between the cases in point; historical exactitude is not required. Since everyone understands that no two historical events can ever truly be exactly the same, the purveyor of historical explanation who claims support from their apparent similarities should have, by far, the easier job in persuasion. It is one thing to argue for there being apparently more or less similarity between or among historical events, it is quite another to claim that two or more sequences of events are all but identical in key features (e.g., plot, victims, aggressors, strategy, tactics, and weapons). Experience and some reflection tell us that claims for strict analogy are rarely appropriate or necessary. The difficult challenge in claiming a precisely common identity between events is so heavy that the temptation and the endeavor are usually best resisted.

An advantage in the use of alleged historical parallels is that if they are employed only occasionally and carefully as to evidence developed in their support, they can prove seriously persuasive. Because the claims for discovery of similarity are so much weaker for the parallel than the allegedly analogous, they are much easier to meet; also, of course, they are near certain not to cover detail that may be vital to the purpose of the argument. The 20th century was richly populated with sequences of like events that had great potential to mislead those most responsible for peace and war in Europe and Asia. Expert familiarity with diplomatic maneuvering in international politics has some ability to mislead the supposedly proficient manipulators for advantage and disadvantage. However, there are limitations even upon the scope of detail guessable by statesmen. What is usually quite beyond the capability of discovery are the possibly vital details of choice that stem from individual personalities and the stimuli they find in a particular context.

Although historical analogies frequently carry an irresistible appeal, readers need to be warned that there are serious perils in analogy. Because they depend upon the plausibility of alleged likeness across many centuries in time and continents in geography, there is often pressure on the author to be generous in his or her interpretation of the events at issue. When an author sets out to write his interpretation of events and their probable meaning over time, it is not to the advantage of the reader for him to act as an advocate on possibly live matters for political argument. Illustration of argument by means of claimed analogy or parallelism can be an effective way to reach an audience who would rather be following their favorite soap operas. It is prudent, however, to remember that the same standard of accuracy does not hold for popular television programs as for scholarly monographs. The main story line and supporting evidence may well be much lighter in the former case, but a historical narrative should not be permitted to tell, or even imply seriously, that events were other than they were known to be, even in popular entertainment. The full story, or some approximation to the truth, may well need to be simplified, but it should not be rewritten for a better cultural fit with the preferences or prejudices of the audience.[16]

The phenomena of claimed historical parallels and analogies are especially at a severe risk of (political) misuse. It is in the nature of these linguistic phenomena to attempt to score political points by being economical with the truth. The reason for using these tricks of speech is to enable the speaker or reader to reach an audience emotionally and typically only to suggest some association between the object of the exercise and potential critics. A few signature jokes may enable a controversial speaker to avoid explaining himself to an audience. Argument by analogy or historical parallel is as unavoidable in a democracy as sometimes it can be extraordinarily effective.

The late and great Harvard professor Samul P. Huntington argued that the United States should behave in a manner that fits its size and importance in the world. He suggested that the country, being extraordinarily large and powerful, should conduct itself in a manner that reflects its potent size and character.

> My basic message is that American strategy and the process by which it is made must reflect the nature of American society. Earlier I criticized those who urged us to adopt a strategy that was at variance with the inherent character of American society.[17]

This could mean that U.S. policy and strategy would tend not so much to rely upon extraordinary skill and finesse, but rather upon superior quantities of material. Huntington did have an important major point to impart. Specifically, a distinguishing feature of the United States is its size and potential as well as its realized strength. This size, and the diversity within it, is a source of some limitations. For example, the country has developed and constructed what is probably the world's finest nuclear arsenal and set of complementary delivery systems. However, this impressive deployment carries the highly unusual caveat that nuclear weapons only have a deterrent function. That characterization is not completely accurate, but it is true enough to cover all cases except any that involve either nuclear threats or which menace vital American (including many Allied) interests. While there has been a constant nuclear military backstop to American statecraft for nearly 70 years, a history of the contribution of nuclear armament to global security and stability will need to look hard to find apparent evidence of the nuclear contribution. This lack of nuclear prominence in our conduct of relations that bear the balance of power may continue indefinitely. Long may it remain so! However, there is an uncertainty about nuclear weapons that should stimulate some modest anxiety. Successful deterrence leaves scant evidence.

Specifically, neither analogy nor parallel offers a helpful way into understanding the perils of a world in which the stability of the global political system depends upon the prudence that should be one of, or possibly the only, guiding quality of statesmen. I am uneasy giving voice to so extreme sounding a point of view, but there is no avoiding the necessity for it in this monograph. There is no historical precedent for a nuclear war. Individual cities have been wiped off the face of the Earth, but a catastrophe without identifiably predictable limits in its destructiveness and longer-term widespread lethal consequences is not a part of human history. Now, this is a possibility. Historical research should be able to help us order our thoughts, including priorities. However, the 72 years since Hiroshima have yielded no obvious source of a nuclear negation that appears to enjoy an extraordinarily high promise of success.

What should the U.S. military learn from the last 7 decades of history about the country's national security? If the first, and potentially overriding, rule in statecraft is prudence, it must follow unavoidably that what the United States has to avoid, almost at all costs, must be any variant of nuclear adventurism. A trouble is that it is the very awesomeness and sheer terror of nuclear war that carries the most telling punch in statecraft.[18] The more acute of the superpower international crises in the era of stable balance, since the mid-1950s, have not yielded a particularly rich haul of nuclear relevant details. Two episodes in particular carried serious danger: Cuba in October 1963 and, for reason of an intelligence failure, the Union of Soviet Socialist Republics in November 1983.[19] The Cuban Missile Crisis soon became famous for common sense, while the Soviet crisis 2 decades later passed undetected in the United States at the time. It is likely that very occasional brief periods of acute technical and operational anxiety have troubled both superpowers. The problem is that we do not know. Because of our ignorance, we have not been able to step back safely from a condition of mutual nuclear deterrence, in order to study recent nuclear near-events calmly. What we think we know is that there is no way in which we could withdraw from our nuclear relationship with Russia. Because of geography and politics, the United States could not prudently leave its NATO commitments. Since there appears to be no technological answer to the threat of nuclear weapons, we are obliged to pursue national security by the political and psychological routes.

The experience of mutual nuclear deterrence can rest for our analysis and understanding only upon the evidence from 60 years or less, which is a distressingly brief period to employ as the basis for the theory and practice of global security. Those of us who have ventured into the locker room of nuclear practice and theory have been periodically worried, perhaps alarmed, by a better appreciation of the awesomely dreadful possibilities. An error in policy, strategy, or tactics by either of the primary protagonists, acting independently or interactively in combination, could have unwelcome consequences almost too grim to consider.

It is extremely difficult to know how best we should prepare for a politically triggered nuclear event that would be far beyond all human experience to date. On war itself, in general, we should feel abundantly well informed, if not misinformed; but bilateral nuclear war of any dimension is completely beyond human experience. The study of history is useful, indeed essential, but when there is no useful data of note, we are compelled to attempt to swim in the dark. It would be somewhat reassuring were we likely to be capable of improving on our performance as a nuclear warfare participant by a consequence of our learning from experience what appears to be successful, politically and strategically, and what does not. However, for better or worse, and unfortunately almost certainly the latter, it appears unlikely that the U.S. Army would be seriously interested in the later phases of a nuclear war, so horrible would any early round almost certainly prove to be. There is an excellent reason why the Army should understand what it can about nuclear warfare, but this is one of those fortunately very rare subjects that does not clarify usably as a consequence of more intense study. There are subjects that appear reluctant to surrender secrets even to the careful military scholar. Possibly, it is fortunate that nuclear conflict with an opponent armed in a manner similar to the United States is not a topic that has attracted much attention of recent years. Probably it is true to claim that an important reason why nuclear warfighting does not attract professional attention more heavily is because of the principles of national security that insist upon the primacy of politics over strategy, and of strategy over tactics. The actual conduct of nuclear warfare would most likely be a near wholly political, and not seriously a military-strategic, exercise. Even if this thought and logic is found less than fully persuasive, in prospect it certainly should have the effect of discouraging strategic imagination.

It is well worth my mentioning as a near certain likelihood the extreme difficulty that would impede analytical or theoretical effort to make strategic sense of nuclear warfare. This is one of those rare cases of an obvious need for strategy where it would not be likely to meet with a strategically sensible response; it would be *terra incognita* for the U.S. Government and Army.

Of course, the preferred answer to the scenario just mentioned has to be a continuation without discernible end of the now longstanding condition of mutual nuclear deterrence. However, a problem with this condition is that it may be vulnerable even to a single failure in the pertinent human, mechanical, and electronic details. In short, our current system of mutual nuclear deterrence could fail catastrophically because of only a very limited breakdown in the supporting human, or the mechanical and electronic systems. The robustness of mutual deterrence should not be doubted. However, the scale of the potential catastrophe is so great that it is only responsible of us to work for a political and military system of international security that has more safety catches than at present.

WHAT CHANGES AND WHAT DOES NOT?

There is a fundamental question lying behind this monograph with which not all of us agree. This is yet another example of the possible potency of assumptions. It is not self-evident that we understand much about military matters that were unknown to Greeks and Romans. Of course, a myriad of detail distinguishes now from then, but it is not obvious that much of deep significance has changed. It is entirely possible that the fundamental premise upon which this monograph is built is unsound. It is possible, and might just be probable, that there is little, if anything, to be learned from the past—distant or near—because we humans are not obviously a species capable of learning from past mistakes.

Many people, perhaps most, seem to believe that change, great and small, is desirable. Often unfortunately, it is welcomed seemingly for its own sake. Because it has become central to the economy of our way of life, the notion of constant change has been allowed to take unsound root. Change, however, is not in itself either prudent or foolish; rather, it must depend on the context. The Armed Forces can appear to believe that a perfectibility of arms is possible. This may be a healthy attitude, even if it always proves to be an ambitious desire too far to reach. The sad truth is that an international arms competition needs to be regarded as a permanent feature of global life, since it can be arrested only by the political force responsible for its creation and growth. So noisy is the clamor from commercial interests and the regular episodic political extravaganzas by means of which we elect political leaders, that it is scarcely surprising to find scant appreciation of our contemporary dependence upon past wisdom and sound practice. A vitally important reason we are able to cast our minds back in confident expectation of discovering examples of prudent behavior, is because quite often we have knowledge of probable historical consequences. When seeking some possible education for the future from the past, we need never to forget that our contemporary ignorance of future consequences has to be regarded as a permanent limitation of any study of the future. The future cannot be studied, in terms either of the largely known past, or of anything else. Zero data is an uncorrectable problem. Zero is still zero, no matter how ingenious social scientific analysis may appear to be. This is disappointing and possibly even discouraging to over-ambitious scientists, but there it is. However, for a notable source of possible assistance, there is the subject of this monograph. It is necessary to be basic, even humble, and enquire of our scholars what they think they know about the future that could be really useful.

Those scholars need to accept an elementary triadic categorization of events of all kinds.

First, there is the past, sometimes as processed selectively by scholars whom we call historians. As the past fades into, and then beyond memory, it is greatly honored with the title of history.[20]

Second, there is the recent passage of time and its abundance of what is known as current affairs. As time passes, first-hand, living knowledge literally expires physically.

Third, there is what commonly is called history. This enormous potential source of knowledge stretches from the outer limit of widespread public first-hand experience and knowledge, all the way back as far as we can reach with our largely archeological findings.

There is certain to be considerable disdain toward troops who proved able to display examples of behavior incompatible with the requirements of a combat ready organization. The U.S. Army, like all others, discovered ancient truths about its soldiers in North Africa and Italy in 1942-43. When the U.S. Army met the German Army in the Mediterranean theater in 1943, the results generally were not flattering to American military self-esteem. The military disadvantage in the comparison made here extended to the very topmost level of command. The overall U.S. military commander, General Dwight D. Eisenhower, had no first-hand combat experience and had never commanded troops in battle prior to his experience in North Africa. Given that his adversaries were German military stars, Albert Kesselring and Erwin Rommel, this imbalance in the quality of leadership was much to the Allied disadvantage. American soldiers needed to learn how to survive and win in combat; being American conveyed no special immunity to harm. In war after war, American soldiers have had to learn to give the enemy of the day the respect they often deserved.[21]

It can be difficult for American soldiers to come to terms with an enemy who needs to be treated with respect, but not by a disabling anxiety or even fear. While American soldiers have been fortunate not to have been compelled by national policy choice to face a truly first-class enemy in the earliest phases of what would become World Wars, it did mean that when the United States eventually became committed to battle it was initially at a severe disadvantage owing to its relative inexperience. American soldiers in 1942 meeting their German adversaries had last met this enemy in the fall of 1918. In addition, the Japanese foe encountered on the Solomon Island of Guadalcanal in 1942 had been fighting already for many preceding years. Moving forward in time, the Viet Cong and North Vietnamese soldiers had many years' experience of battle, before the U.S. Army entered South Vietnam in large numbers in 1965.

There is an assertion of historical change that is no better than a plausible fallacy. Change in conditions, tools, and beliefs have been a fact beyond doubt. That fact, however, cannot just be assumed to have great significance. It does not usually require much historical scholarship to enable us to appreciate the difference between major and minor causes of change. Furthermore, the number of the latter is easy to exaggerate. While cultural, including moral, change is relatively rare and indeed tends to be negated and reversed as a consequence of its negative results, material change can be rapid and difficult to assimilate and, if necessary, adopt. Ideational change typically is more of a challenge to master and overcome than is material change. Whereas material discovery, technological innovation, and novel practices can be routinized by a scientifically advanced society, cultural change at the level of revolution tends to be far more difficult for people to comprehend and then practice.

Soldiers in the U.S. Army reading this monograph may notice that the nonmaterial difference between today and ancient times are easily exaggerated. The essence of strategy applied as directly and consequentially for Greeks, Romans, and Persians, as it does for us today and, we can predict confidently, will do so tomorrow. The unforgiving core logic of strategy has not altered over time. Indeed, changes in weaponry and logistical provision scarcely signify for mention when they are contrasted with the major causes of strategic strife that have scarcely changed at all over millennia. The risks and rewards in soldiers' lives assuredly have been cumulatively altered quite a bit over the centuries, but the enduring and fundamental logic of strategy always applies, notwithstanding the wide range in the detail of historical variation.

For conceptual clarification, sound understanding of military behavior in any period should flow from a view of history in terms of the relations among just four master concepts—ends, ways, means, and assumptions. Historical actors in any and every period have been obliged by contextual necessity to endeavor to cope with the relations among the imperative logic of these four key ideas. The four concepts are strictly architectural in their logic; they can explain historical failure as well as success. The great changes that undoubtedly have occurred emphatically have not weakened the basic logical sense in the necessary cooperative connections that should unify ends, ways, means, and assumptions.

The principal benefit of the formula of ends, ways, means, and assumptions naturally does not lie in any particular mastery of historical narrative. Instead, it equips the soldier as a warrior scholar, or simply as an interested general reader, adequately for understanding how and why military power can, and perhaps should, work.[22] Whoever the enemy, whatever the terrain, and regardless of the detail of political intention, there is need for: clarity in political purpose; a requirement for sufficiently effective ways to threaten and apply force; and a need to be matched by adequate means to achieve the necessary application.

For the purpose of this monograph, it is necessary for the reader to accept as a possible, I believe certain, fact a quite startling contrast. On the one hand, a world expressing and reflecting minor and major change in many features and circumstances. On the other hand, in contrast, there is the plain evidence of a near steady state in the values that have much deeper meaning and reflect lasting worth. Unsurprisingly, the more senior the level of command, the more readily comparable have been the possible and probable lessons of history. It would be more accurate to follow Sir Michael Howard when he draws a distinction between history simply as the past, and history meaning the past as massaged and interpreted by historians.[23]

Looking back, even over a very long time, some immediate tentative conclusions press for consideration. For example, if we consider Roman military experience we discover that the experience at different ranks of contrasting responsibilities bear strong similarities between then and now. At the topmost level, the tools employed have changed hugely, indeed beyond recognition, but the challenges have not altered greatly. The general officer still acts on behalf of the state, and is held responsible if policy is shown by field experience not to have been chosen wisely. In addition, the military leader will find today that he needs to be able to lead as well as command, and that not all of his most senior subordinate officers are fully competent. In some cases, this will pose a serious difficulty when the senior commanders in question have politically heavy hitting potential support. This difficult case arises when at (our) home or when they are appointed to satisfy strong domestic interests or meet a strong foreign interest.

Of course, the soldiers willing to learn from their country's history may discover that there is, or could be, a path to political authority, paved by the natural popularity of military success. Whether fully merited or not, truly outstanding military leaders in the

United States do have a history of post-war democratic political success. George Washington, Zachary Taylor, Ulysses S. Grant, Dwight Eisenhower, and even possibly David Petraeus spring to mind as the outstanding exemplars of this phenomenon, even though a yearning for political power was not a life-long defining characteristic of all of them. What is required here above all else is education in the theory and practice of connections among the increasingly elevated levels of conflict. Soldiers need to understand, even if occasionally only resentfully, that all of the combat in warfare, and all the logistical effort involved, can only be justified in terms of its net achievement. It can have no justification, even meaning, if it is not firmly connected to higher purposes. Whenever and wherever one looks in historical records, all military activity, in times of peace or of war, has to serve a purpose of a nature different from its own. The American military person should realize that he or she represents but the latest human example of a great historical truth. Specifically, military power of all kinds has some political meaning. That is not a matter for policy choice. The military institution is, and has to be, about politics, even though it is not itself political in its nature.

Some historical perspective frequently is asked and even expected of our political leaders, though often, indeed usually, people forget about the genuine limitations on our knowledge. Recognition of such limitations should be an important step on the path of improvement in historical utility. For example, there is no way in which either acute crisis or the outbreak of war can be predicted by the harder or the softer sciences. There is no miracle formula that can unravel the relevant mysteries of the future. However, careful analysis of past crises and political-military competitions enable us to identify conditions of unusual peril. Because of our eternal ignorance of what will happen later today, let alone tomorrow and thereafter, we need strictly to follow a rule of prudence in international security affairs. Knowledge of the past cannot serve a reliable predictive purpose, but it should alert us to understanding what can happen. Since we must assume that there is great continuity in human history, we are obliged to assume that what has occurred may be repeated, albeit in rather more modern forms. Bearing in mind the awesome dangers of nuclear holocaust, and the grossly incomplete success achieved to date with regard to the alleviation of interstate armed conflict, it is only prudent for us to seek such assistance as may be sought from history.

WHAT CAN THE U.S. ARMY LEARN FROM HISTORY?

An attempt such as this, to identify ideas and behavior from history may be, certainly may appear to be, wildly overambitious. I have chosen to identify and explain just eight conclusions that I have reached as a consequence of my more than 50 years of scholarship, much of it on matters that bear closely upon the national security of the United States. The question in the title to the topic of this monograph could prove impracticably large, almost beyond discipline. As a consequence of the boundary resistant concept of history I have been obliged to exercise ruthless judgment with respect to inclusion and exclusion of subjects. What follows is a relatively brief discussion of a modest number of answers to the large question set by the U.S. Army War College (USAWC) and the Strategic Studies Institute (SSI). I have decided not to attempt to provide a descending order of relative significance, because an effort to do this could mislead the reader by encouraging him or her to think in terms of fairly orderly categories. However, the past, present, and future is not like that. Events of all kinds often just occur when they do. Real life in all ages often surprises participants; the past truly is disorderly, despite the energetic efforts of some people and institutions, everywhere and always, to plan and enable orderly and purposeful progress. When we are advised to try to make sense of history, what is meant is the sense already discovered. My argument is that even the most planned and controlled of human endeavors will have a tendency, assuredly a potential, to go off the rails and descend into a variant of chaos. I am not talking mainly about willful mischief, but rather about our human capability to make mistakes, become confused, or simply be individualistic in a world that has expectations and a requirement for us to obey rules that are orders. Military institutions, in particular, understand well and appropriately that they live and perform almost literally on the edge of chaos. The history of all countries, especially when they engage in armed conflict—in any period in the past—usually is a story both of struggle against an identified enemy, but also against error and confusion in their own ranks. This tendency toward, indeed some need to tolerate, disorder was almost a quality required of the U.S. Army in the 20th century, as twice it needed to grow exponentially in order to do battle with first Imperial, then Nazi, Germany. On both occasions, in 1917-18 and 1942-43, the U.S. Army had the best of reasons to be grateful that Allied armies already, if ironically, had been well trained by their common German enemy.

The analysis and choice of evidence employed in this section of this monograph has been carefully selected to minimize the possibility of bias in the text. The frequency with which British and American cases are cited reflects nothing more sinister than the author's professional foci over half a century of study. It is worth mentioning that I believe nearly all the arguments and major points registered in the following section are quite general truths that apply to the national security systems of many countries.

1. Interpreting the Past, a Basic Question of Context and Authority

The past is owned by nobody; history, in sharpest contrast, bears many claims to ownership. These claims appear mainly in the writings of professional historians; these scholars may tell the truth about the past that they know. However, that truth is certain to depend upon a limited and particular empirical base of evidence and also upon the authors' preferences that reflect various motivations. The historian writing history is not a scholar faithfully transcribing words that bear a divine authority. Instead, they reflect a selection of knowledge the historian has allowed himself to see and consider, as well as the facts to which he, or she, did not have reliable access. Truth about the past may have rotted away in the course of time, been heedlessly damaged or destroyed, or hidden by accident or design by people many years ago. All works of what commonly is called history lack authority to a greater or lesser degree. Unavoidably, they will not and cannot know the truth as it was understood in the past by historical figures. This is not to criticize historians; their problem, as well as possible advantage, is one of perspective and that derives critically from particular context.

As Professor Sir Michael Howard argued:

> history, whatever its value in educating the judgement, teaches no 'lessons,' and the professional historians will be as skeptical of those who claim that it does as professional doctors are of their colleagues who peddle medicines guaranteeing instant cures.[24]

A universal fact so obvious that it usually escapes notice and attention is in need of recognition. Everyone, in all periods, enjoys or endures what is known as context. This potent concept captures in meaning all that is known and understood by a person including those forces and influences that shape circumstances, whether or not they are recognized at the time. Context shares much in common with the idea of assumptions. Both concepts are incredibly powerful, yet attract little explicit scholarly or popular attention. The concepts of context and assumptions are of great significance for this study, because in mutually dependent ways they both have profound meaning for many, indeed most, claims concerning the motives of historical actors. Many of life's decisions rest upon assumptions that we do not feel any need to challenge, sometimes even when we would be at liberty to do so.

It would be a non-trivial challenge to ask of an American soldier today that he or she should attempt to think as soldiers in times possibly long past. Probably it would be a greater challenge to ask of American soldiers that they ought to try to recognize and learn from the experience of other soldiers, possibly foreign and long dead. No matter how surprising it may be to many of today's soldiers, relatively little about military planning, combat itself, logistics, and communications is a revelation revealed only by the awesomely awful global military history of the past century. Nonetheless, of course the tactical and technical details of change matter profoundly at the sharpest end of military life and sometimes death. However, much of what has been, and remains, of great strategic significance has scarcely altered at all in its essentials over the centuries. This is an important reason why we can still read Greek and Roman authors with sympathy and even gratitude.

2. The Human Race Has Not Learned Sufficiently from Its History — Yet!

It is both a prudent and a sad truth about this assertion that it does not inspire any particular kind of behavior by the military student. A trouble with history, in the sense of an ever-arguable narrative, is that it is prudently safe because by definition it is about the past. This is neither to forget nor deny that the past already may have been mortgaged for the future. However, its substance, even if seriously regretted by some today, is done and gone for better or worse. However, since past behavior cannot be recalled and returned in hope of our achieving an improved outcome, we are obliged by the laws of physics only to perform a single journey into the future. Therefore, acting as two complementary inhibitors, knowledge and understanding of the future is hampered severely by an inability to predict the future reliably in detail. Certainly, we are able to, and do, predict; but ambitious predictions are hardly ever beyond risk of serious error. Leaving aside the large issue of the readiness of historical knowledge for useful raiding by scholars in need of assistance, there is usually considerable room for disagreement over the wisdom of important choices in the past. It is one thing to assert that a particular choice in our history had researchable, identifiable consequences; it is quite another to argue there were some unwelcome alternatives that were not tried.

The second point about learning from history tends not to be made by cameras with a width of lens at all suitable to the subject. "The paths not taken" is likely to provide material for extensive study. This logic inclines us to be more tolerant of theoretical alternative courses of action than soldiers often are able to be, prudently. When a decision for action or inaction is needed this day, possibly this hour or even this minute, understanding possible alternatives is more likely to paralyze than to assist. Moving up the ladder of likely consequences, from tactical through operational, to strategic and eventually political choice, many strategic decisions have literally unknowable and certainly unpredictable results. In addition, just as few, if any, major strategic decisions will be free of greater or lesser risk, so ambitious governments must be able to tolerate bad military and political news.

All countries "cherry pick" particular items from the whole library of preferred national history. Everyone — all cultures — can find examples of national heroism against the odds. All countries have a tale or two of struggles against adversity; for example, defeat that is really a moral victory, as with the Alamo in 1836, or Wake Island, and Bataan in 1942. There has been ample genuine heroism in the global human story. There is no need to mention the fact that grim tales of extraordinary military effort for survival exist in all countries' histories, legends, and mythologies. History textbooks are not weighed around the world in order to ascertain the probable truth they seek to convey to the young.

Anyway, who or which institution could be trusted to tell the truth, if — that is — the truth is a valid ambition. All countries have a vested interest in telling their history largely from the biased perspective of themselves. The historical education of the young everywhere is, in varying degree, tribal. This is readily understandable and indeed inevitable and unavoidable, though it is hardly praiseworthy.

3. Bad Times Always Return

History does not repeat itself, but one cannot avoid noticing that there would appear to be a repetitive, if somewhat irregular, pattern to conditions of peace and war. Especially noticeable is the repetition of threat on a major scale to the integrity of the United States for much of the country's relatively brief existence. Eras of peace and tranquility have not often been the lot of Americans; whether our security concerns were more or less confined to North America, which was the case in the 18th and 19th centuries. Addressing problems of national security in a global context, the American experience since 1900 has been exciting and dangerous. A condition literally of extreme peril has now become the situation normal for Americans in an era of nuclear weapons. This reality of life in the shadow of nuclear danger, seemingly, has all but lost the power to shock, so habituated are we to the danger.

A careful reading of history leads unavoidably to the conclusion that bad times always return. This is a fact based on ample evidence from all periods in the past of our species. The soldier reading works of history will be at risk of misunderstanding much that is controversial, even essentially unknowable with total confidence, but that should not much matter. What should matter for the soldier is to appreciate those conditions of instability and insecurity most likely to continue long into the future. There has been no philosophy, religion, or political ideology proved able to unite all of mankind. It has not happened, period! Given what we think we know and understand about past millennia, alas, it is a completely safe bet that the human race will not improve. All we can do is be vigilant on our watch.

4. In the Hierarchy of Professional Concern to Soldiers, Policy and its Politics are More Important than Strategy, Operations, and Tactics

As a student of strategy for more than 50 years, I find this rather a challenge to write. It should be a standard truth that professional soldiers do not question legitimate orders issued by their political superiors that were transmitted through the proper chain of command. That said, it is plausible to argue that inappropriate political choices are the principal culprits in many cases. Sometimes, fortunately rarely, there is a cause for war so serious that the country has little discretion in its choice of response, or even initiative. Most polities occasionally confront the necessity for making an unwelcome choice. It is important to remember that even a country as uniquely powerful as the United States can find itself in a strategic and therefore also a political situation that appears to admit of no alternative answers to the politically existential question posed: Do we fight? This was the grim prospect in South Korea in June 1950, while much more arguably it had been the case also in 1917 and 1940-41.

The argument of greatest relative significance here is that political choices typically, even many untypically, can have a weight in consequences that more narrow ones cannot reach. Though often only with much embarrassment, and certainly a great deal of pain, there are no decisions at the rare level of national policy, with its politics, that could not change sharply the course taken by the nation. The simple seeming staff college model of ends, ways, and means (with appropriate assumptions), really in its profound meaning says it all! The political goals that are policy ends, the strategic ways to achieve them, and the various (including military) means to behave as may be required should not confuse the student. The military institutions of the state ought to be able to advise and, if necessary, warn political authorities about the likely consequences of their policy choices. However, it is only exceptional for a major political choice leading to large-scale warfare to be challenged, even retroactively in such popular democracies as the United States and the United Kingdom. The British Chilcot Enquiry into the Iraq War, which took 8 years to conduct and complete, was a notable exception to the usual rule that efforts are not made to seek out and apportion responsibility, and therefore blame, for policy choices that subsequent developments show to have been a mistake. By far the most important conclusion we should draw from the enquiry led by Lord Chilcot was about the significance of political choice, not so much about British military competence in Iraq, which undoubtedly was less than stellar. Soldiers may well make the best of a job that ought to have been deemed too difficult for them to attempt. High tactical and even operational competence will not suffice to compensate for fatally poor political choices in policy. Even excellence in policy offers no guarantee of advantage; it cannot compensate adequately for basic errors in policy choice. There may be local and temporary benefit to be gained through tactical and even operational superiority, but that is unlikely to lead to an enduring advantage; for that to be the case one must look to politics.

5. Predictions and Assumptions About War Should Never Be Trusted Uncritically

By definition, predictions and assumptions are made even though there is a lack of empirical evidence in their support. Because of our incapability to see over the time horizon to the future, we need to make many decisions that can rest only on preparation, not real-time experience. The individual soldier knows how high the personal risk can be in warfare, but he or she does not know, and fortunately cannot predict, how severe the danger will prove to be. What the soldier will not know is how great a strategic, and therefore political, risk the country is taking in a decision for war. What the soldier, conscript, or volunteer is unlikely to know, or possibly even understand, is the abundantly evidenced worldwide truth that war is always a gamble. So many and intense are the calculations and emotions that go into a war that a really confident prediction about results, let alone consequences, should always be treated with suspicion. The course and outcome of war often turn out to be surprising to the belligerents. Actions for and within war assuredly can be planned and much should be predictable, but the live, real-time dynamics of warfare invariably are a mystery ahead of time. The fundamental reason for this is the existence of a self-willed enemy. Neat and effective plans that largely ignore the will and capability of the enemy are dangerous. Strategic intentions that simply assume away any inconvenient competence on the part of the enemy are all too familiar. We can recall the French folly concerning the assumption that the Viet-Minh would lack the ability to mount a serious artillery threat to the garrison of Dien Bien Phu in 1954.[25] A decade earlier, there was the convenient assumption by General Mark Clark that German General Albert Kesselring's Luftwaffe posed no serious threat from the air to the Allied amphibious operation at Salerno south of Rome.[26] We do not want to discourage American soldiers from taking risks, but we need to teach or remind them that decisions for war, great or small, are always a gamble; they will be a move beyond empirical evidence.

6. Of Course Battles Matter, but Typically Wars are Won or Lost Strategically and Politically

Single, allegedly decisive battles are a rarity in the entire narrative of history.[27] They do occur, but it is more common for a great clash of arms in battle to be only a bloody episode in the entire narrative of a conflict. Popular fiction and movies thrive on little nourishment from a fairly thin list of battles that were probably more terrifying events for the participants than they were strategically meaningful. Readers may recall that this monograph insisted much earlier that strategy essentially is about the consequences of action. In modern times—say since the founding of the American Republic in 1776—it has been rare for a belligerent to roll the dice in battle in a decisively concluding move. The reasons are not hard to identify; two such are technology and ideology. The range and therefore reach of national military power, thinking of air, missile, and also of nuclear weapons, has rendered war a potentially history-ending experience. This menace poses insoluble difficulties for states. It is quite a challenge to be in a condition of war-readiness, indeed of an approximate hair-trigger alertness for a long period, when the war we threaten to inflict would not be survivable. This last claim may not be reliably true. Obviously, evidence is missing, but we would be suitably prudent to assume it is true. If we seek strategic advantage for political gain, as probably we should very rarely, there can be no forgetting the nuclear peril that could conclude the American experience.

7. History is not a Morality Tale

Many factors enhance the prospect of national success, but a moral advantage is not credibly among them. When a government or political elite commits crimes against all of humanity today, it may pay a heavy price in terms of political support denied. A modern electorate will be capable of punishing unsuccessful candidates by excluding them from positions of political power. The moral audit of thought and behavior typically does not carry sanctions more painful than exclusion from high office. However, soldiers seeking to learn from history will discover that democracy with a universal adult franchise has not been the norm in the past. They learn also that in most countries for long periods it was physically dangerous to lead politically. In particular periods, the 3rd century A.D. for example, it was unusual for a Roman emperor to die peacefully.

A concept as non-specific as the past plainly can accommodate virtually every claimed exception to whatever otherwise is claimed to have been a familiar informal rule governing human political and moral behavior and misbehavior. Governments do not like to be caught out by journalists, let alone by a court of international law, for having committed undoubtable wrongdoing when they are ethically regarded. However, even less do they favor an undeniable failure of policy. A problem is that the standard of right (enough) conduct has varied over the centuries, as has the freedom of action of political leaders. There is little room for doubt that the difference between success and failure is as clear today as it was in antiquity. The actual content of the two contrasting ideas has varied richly over time and in different circumstances, but still the two usually are distinguishable.

It is plausible to claim that right conduct by contemporary standards has hardly ever been allowed a dominant role in political decision-making. Nonetheless, few political leaders have been genuinely and repeatedly indifferent to moral condemnation. Readers of history soon notice, however, that nearly all major policy decisions in most countries in every period of history have been both praised and condemned. Inevitably, this means that even when there appear to have been plain cases of immoral behavior, there were, almost certainly, some mighty arguments that could be advanced in justification. Overall, one is obliged by the empirical evidence to conclude that political leaders tend overwhelmingly to follow a pragmatic rule of contemporary expediency.

8. Great Powers Can Make Great Mistakes

As in individual interpersonal relations, governments are capable of making mistakes. Obviously, the greater the state in question, the larger and consequentially more deleterious the mistakes in policy choice are likely to be. The reason is that nearly all of the larger choices in public policy could be argued in different ways. Often it is quite a challenge for the historian to be sufficiently emotionally detached from the historical circumstances under examination. They need to retain the necessary distance for adequate objectivity. Historians often become surrogate participants in policy controversies of the past, sometimes even the long past. An obvious and unavoidable problem with a historian as a kind of participant advocate for one side or another is that they are both blessed and cursed with possession of the priceless pearl of foreknowledge about yesterday's future. While there can be high value in determining the probable consequences of actions taken at a certain date, it can be fiendishly difficult for us to avoid using our knowledge from the future improperly.

The larger the country, the larger major errors in policy are likely to be, and the deeper and longer lasting the likely consequences of ill-chosen policy. The three most recent examples of well-intentioned American policy that deserved to succeed—Vietnam, Afghanistan, and Iraq—unsurprisingly perhaps, generated warfare of a character that was locally all but uniformly unfortunate. In all three historic cases just cited, the fundamental problem for the United States was of the same kind: weakness in the understanding of local politics and culture. From time to time, an expeditionary intervention led by the United States may be timely and advisable. However, such extreme action should not be taken largely in the vague hope that things will turn out acceptably. The United States should only commit to military action when it understands what it is doing, why it is doing it, and how policy objectives are to be secured. Some mistakes are inevitable, but many in the recent past were foresee-able, and therefore should have been avoidable.

RECOMMENDATIONS FOR THE U.S. ARMY

1. Behave Prudently

Prudent behavior is that which is conducted with careful regard for the future. Strategy is all about con-sequences. The past is already done and gone, poorly or well and usually some of both. The constant need to insist that soldiers today act with appreciation of the high relevance of prudence in thought and action aims at the very heart of strategy. Many people, including scholars, need reminding that military action has no positive value in and of itself. The very idea of con-sequences can often appear irrelevant, because the challenge today is so demanding that military com-manders find no time, or spare energy, to devote to possible happenings in the future. It is understandable if they feel so fully employed trying to meet current demands that they lack the spare personal capacity needed for worry about tomorrow. Of course, it is not always obvious which is the most prudent course of action to adopt, especially given that an undue deter-mination to behave prudently risks having to meet with the charge of being unduly cautious. That said, as it needs to be, there is a general need for prudence, meaning the holding to a serious concern about the consequences of a chosen action.

2. Remember the Concept of the Great Stream of Time

It is healthy for personal humility, even if, indeed perhaps particularly if, they are senior generals, not to forget that they and their behavior has meaning in, and consequences for, the great stream of time for the human past, or history.[28] There can be high utility in understanding clearly that there is little done today that could not be repudiated, overturned, or even reversed tomorrow. More than casual acknowledgement of that possible fact should encourage some respect for the taking of a longer view of history than otherwise might be the case. It is important, even critically so, not to forget that only a nuclear military event offers the highly plausible prospect of, quite literally, an end to history of any interest to us today. Almost anything and everything else can be accommodated for consequential historical meaning. The concept of the great stream of time has room for both good and bad news. It has been said many times that there is a great deal of ruin in a nation; meaning in this instance that the United States has a national government that makes both good and less good decisions. Although a particular national administration will make regrettable decisions that have unfortunate consequences that were not foreseen, presidencies come and go on the 4-year cycle. At least, happily, this is the American way in politics and governance.

3. War Is Always a Policy Gamble

So many and so unpredictable are the factors that operate in war, that high confidence prior to hostilities is likely to prove ill founded. It is a problem for the

United States that its own status and capabilities are so high. It can prove almost impossibly challenging for Americans to understand just how much, or how little, military effort to exert in order to bring a local conflict to a successful conclusion. Since 1945, the U.S. Army has drawn one conflict in Korea, undoubtedly lost another in Vietnam, and at best has not obviously succeeded in two others in Afghanistan and Iraq. In the negative cases just cited, the core of the Army's problem set was the same; it was committed to combat in a country that was culturally too alien for it to be able to convert its tactical prowess into meaningful strategic gain for political purpose. The political purpose is what the exercise of American military power has to be about. In war after war, from the 1960s to the 2000s, the U.S. Army was partially engaged in countries whose cultures and even politics were substantially mysterious to America's political leaders and most American voters. This extensive and intensive asymmetry contributed hugely to U.S. military and political failure in South-East Asia and the Middle East. Strange to say, perhaps, but war—any war—is always a political gamble. This is as true for a superpower as for states much smaller than the United States. The general strength of this point is probably less than—let alone fully—well understood, even in the U.S. Army. The extensive and genuine military virtue of this Army ironically may hinder comprehension of its relative weakness when it strives to counter hostilities significantly foreign to Americans. Policy decisions to commit the U.S. Army to a war are always going to be highly risky, because of the large number and character of uncertainties.

4. War Should Only Be Waged with Strategic Sense.

It is a vitally important definitional truth that war ought only and always to be waged with what some insightful historians have termed "strategic sense."[29] There should be no misunderstanding of the relative importance and significance of this recommendation to the Army. Tactics and even operations will be the regular actuality of military behavior of the U.S. Army in a zone of conflict, but we must never lose sight of the whole political point of the death, destruction, and disturbance that we cause and promote. In an army such as the American where politics is eschewed, as well as unprofessional, it can prove difficult for the military strategy to remain apolitical. This strategy should cap and exploit tactics and operations, but not leak or stray into the realm of policy with its ineradicable politics. Despite the legal and professional cultural inhibitions that always will work overtime to be difficult, there can be no prudent way in which to seek to escape the necessity for the U.S. Army only to be wielded as a sharp military instrument in execution or support of a clear political purpose. The separation of the military from the world of politics is a deep and important value in American public culture. Nonetheless, the separation cannot be permitted to license, if not actually encourage, a foolish distancing of our Army's actions from our society's high political and moral intentions.

ENDNOTES

1. L. P. Hartley, *The Go-Between*, Harmondsworth, UK: Penguin Books, 1953, p. 7.

2. Michael Howard, *The Lessons of History*, New Haven, CT: Yale University Press, 1991, p. 11; see also John Vincent, *History*, New York: Continuum, 1995.

3. The first book in Rick Atkinson's *Liberation Trilogy* tells a story of an over expanded U.S. Army that was no match for the Wehrmacht in North Africa, but was fortunate to be opposed primarily by Italians in the earliest campaigns in the Mediterranean theater. See Rick Atkinson, *An Army at Dawn: The War in North Africa, 1942–1943*, New York: Henry Holt, 2002. It is only fair to comment that the British 8th Army, which had been fighting Rommel all the way from Egypt, was not dramatically more effective in opposing the Germans than were the Americans, notwithstanding the success at El Alamein. German military leadership was in a class unmatched by the Allies. It was fortunate that the lion's share of the German Army was more than fully engaged in Russia.

4. Amidst a large number of useful books, see W. V. Harris, *Roman Power: A Thousand Years of Empire*, Cambridge, UK: Cambridge University Press, 2016.

5. Thucydides, *The Landmark Thucydides: A Comprehensive Guide to the Peloponnesian War*, Robert B. Strassler, ed. and rev. trans., Richard Crawley (1876), New York: The Free Press, 1996.

6. Paul A. Rahe, "Thucydides as Educator," in Williamson Murray and Richard Hart Sinnreich, eds., *The Past as Prologue: The Importance of History to the Military Profession*, Cambridge, UK: Cambridge University Press, 2006, pp. 99–100.

7. Norman H. Gibbs, "Clausewitz and the Moral Forces in War," *Naval War College Review*, Vol. VII, No. 4, January/February 1975, pp. 15-22.

8. See the important short article by T. X. Hammes, "Assumptions—A Fatal Oversight," *Infinity Journal*, Vol. 1, Winter 2010, pp. 4-6.

9. The virtues of prudence for the guidance of statecraft are propounded in Raymond Aron, *Peace and War: A Theory of International Relations*, New York: Doubleday, 1966, p. 285.

10. See Linda Robinson, Paul D. Miller, John Gordon IV, Jeffrey Decker, Michael Schwille, and Raphael S. Cohen, *Improving Strategic Competence: Lessons from 13 Years of War*, Santa Monica, CA: RAND Corporation, 2014. The RAND authors did not sugar

the pill they offered: "Lesson 1: The making of national security strategy has suffered from a lack of understanding and application of strategic art," p. xii.

11.   Carl von Clausewitz, *On War*, Michael Howard and Peter Paret, eds. and trans., Princeton, NJ: Princeton University Press, 1976, pp. 80-81, is helpfully uncompromising in its treatment of the "political object" in war. Also, see Donald Stoker, *The Grand Design: Strategy and the U.S. Civil War*, New York: Oxford University Press, 2010.

12.   Robinson *et al.*, p. 33.

13.   Two books by Bernard Brodie made especially significant impact on the understanding of the strategic meaning of the nuclear revolution: Bernard Brodie, *Strategy in the Missile Age*, Princeton, NJ: Princeton University Press, 1959; and Bernard Brodie, *War and Politics*, New York, Macmillan, 1973. A notable work from a different part of the strategy and policy spectrum is Robert Jervis, *The Meaning of the Nuclear Revolution: Statecraft and the Prospect of Armageddon*, Ithaca, NY: Cornell University Press, 1989.

14.   See Stoker. The final sentence in this book deserves a wide audience (p. 418):

> The Union triumphed in the end because it managed to develop strategic responses that addressed the nature of this particular war and the character of this particular enemy and then set about implementing them for as long as it took to achieve their political objectives. The Confederacy never did — and perished.

15.   See H. W. Fowler, *A Dictionary of Modern English Usage*, Hertfordshire, UK: Wordsworth Editions Limited, 1994, pp. 20-22, 295-296.

16.   On the public uses and particularly the abuses of history, see Jeremy Black, *The Curse of History*, London, UK: The Social Affairs Unit, 2008.

17.   Samuel P. Huntington, "American Military Strategy," *Policy Papers in International Affairs*, No. 28, Berkeley, CA: Institute of International Studies, University of California, Berkeley, 1986.

18. See Herman Kahn, *On Thermonuclear War*, Princeton, NJ: Princeton University Press, 1960.

19. See the excellent Cold War history written by an author who was an insider in British Intelligence, Gordon S. Barrass, *The Great Cold War: A Journey Through the Hall of Mirrors*, Stanford, CA: Stanford University Press, 2009, ch. 28.

20. The most enlightening treatment of the role and status of the professional historian remains Howard, ch. 1.

21. For three variations on a theme see Colin S. Gray, *The Strategy Bridge: Theory for Practice*, Oxford, UK: Oxford University Press, 2010; Beatrice Heuser, *The Evolution of Strategy: Thinking War from Antiquity to the Present*, Cambridge, UK: Cambridge University Press, 2010; and Lawrence Freedman, *Strategy: A History*, Oxford, UK: Oxford University Press, 2013.

22. See Clausewitz, pp. 133-147; and Harry R. Yarger, *Strategy and the National Security Professional: Strategic Thinking and Strategy Formulation in the 21st Century*, Westport, CT: Praeger Security International, 2008.

23. Howard, espec., pp. 11-13.

24. *Ibid.*, p. 11.

25. Martin Windrow, *The Last Valley: Dien Bien Phu and the French Defeat in Vietnam*, London, UK: Weidenfeld and Nicolson, 2004.

26. See Rick Atkinson, *The Day of Battle: The War in Sicily and Italy, 1943–1944*, New York: Henry Holt, 2007, p. 217.

27. See Colin S. Gray, *Defining and Achieving Decisive Victory*, Carlisle, PA: Strategic Studies Institute, U.S. Army War College, April 2002.

28. For a superior guide to this major, indeed rather intimidating concept, see Richard E. Neustadt and Ernest R. May, *Thinking in Time: The Uses of History for Decision-Makers*, New York: The Free Press, 1986.

29. Robert Lyman, *The Generals: From Defeat to Victory, Leadership in Asia 1941–45*, London, UK: Constable, 2008, p. 341.

U.S. ARMY WAR COLLEGE

Major General William E. Rapp
Commandant

*****

STRATEGIC STUDIES INSTITUTE
AND
U.S. ARMY WAR COLLEGE PRESS

Director
Professor Douglas C. Lovelace, Jr.

Director of Research
Dr. Steven K. Metz

Author
Dr. Colin S. Gray

Editor for Production
Dr. James G. Pierce

Publications Assistant
Ms. Denise J. Kersting

*****

Composition
Mrs. Jennifer E. Nevil

FOR THIS AND OTHER PUBLICATIONS, VISIT US AT

armywarcollege.edu

ISBN 1-58487-763-4

9 781584 877639

90000>

This Publication

SSI Website

USAWC Website

www.ingramcontent.com/pod-product-compliance
Lightning Source LLC
Chambersburg PA
CBHW081243250726
48654CB00012B/1457